I0759718

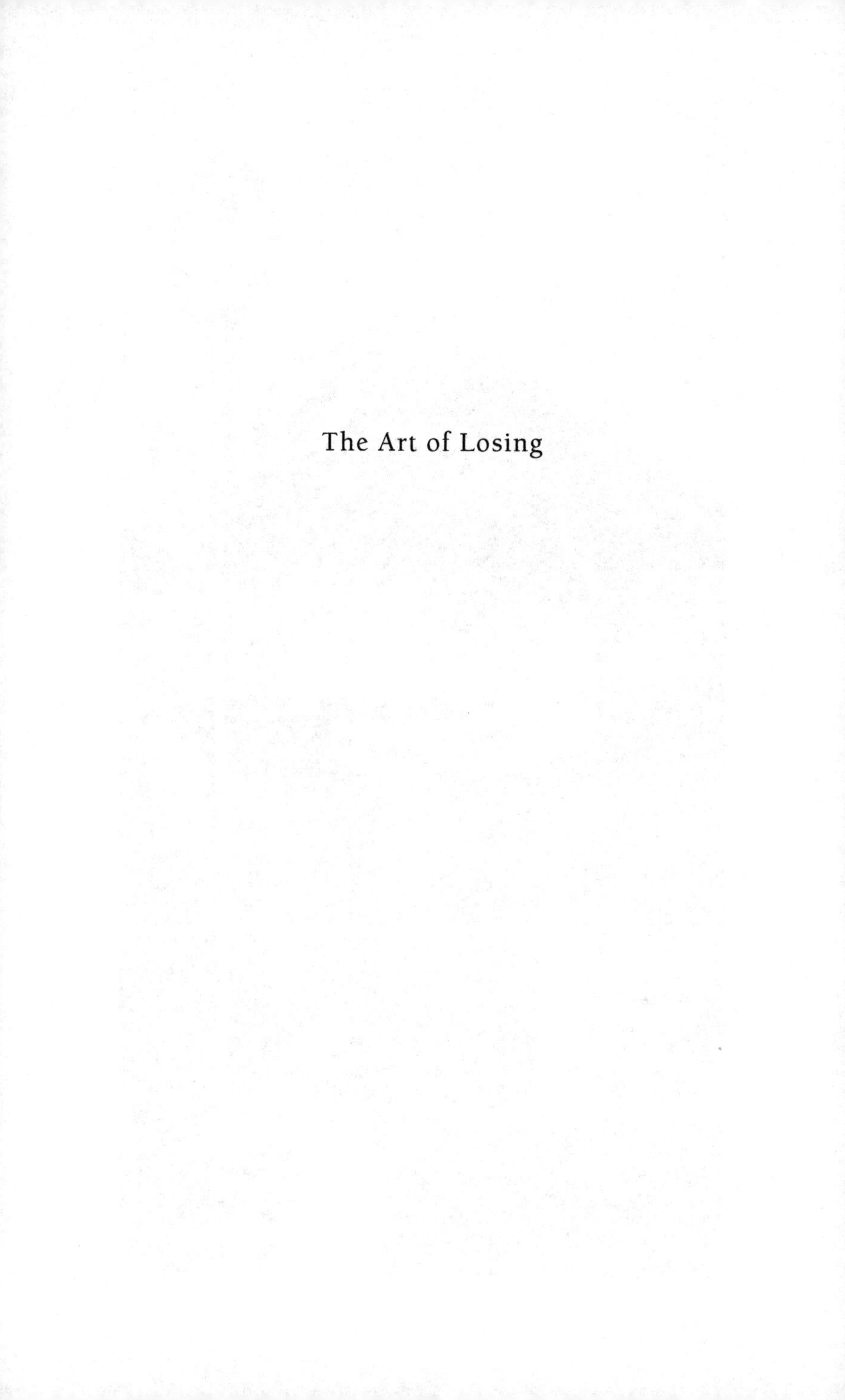

The Art of Losing

The Art of Losing

Twelve Poems on
Grief and Consolation

M. WYNN THOMAS
Illustrations by Ruth Jên Evans

2025

www.uwp.co.uk

British Library CIP Data

A catalogue record for this book is available from the British Library.

ISBN: 978-1-83760-023-6
eISBN: 978-1-83760-026-7

The publisher acknowledges the financial support of the Books Council of Wales

Printed and bound by CPI Group (UK) Ltd, Croydon, CR0 4YY

For all General Product Safety Regulation (GPSR) enquiries, please contact: Logos Europe, 9 rue Nicolas Poussin, 17000, La Rochelle, France contact@logoseurope.eu

Er cof am mam a 'nhad yn bennaf
Ond hefyd am y llu eraill 'a gerais
gynt ond collais ennyd awr'

In memory of my mother and father,
but also of the many I 'have loved
long since but lost awhile'

Nid yw yfory yn difa hiraeth,
Nac ymwroli'n nacáu marwolaeth,
Fe ddeil pangfeydd ei alaeth – tra bo co',
Ei dawn i wylo yw gwerth dynoliaeth.

Tomorrow does not erase longing,
Nor bravado cancel out death,
The pangs of grief last long as memory,
The gift of weeping is humanity's core.

DIC JONES
(1934–2009)
from 'Galarnad'
on the death of his daughter Esyllt,
a child with Down's syndrome,
at the age of three (my translation).

Contents

Prefatory Note

the art of losing's not too hard to master
though it may look like (*Write* it!) like disaster.

This is the concluding couplet of 'One Art', a villanelle by the distinguished American poet Elizabeth Bishop. It encapsulates the several distinct aspects, or perhaps phases, of the human experience of grieving. First, there is the reflex action to protect oneself against the pain through, perhaps, wry understatement and artful irony. Then, there is the inescapable necessity of facing up to it and accepting its devastatingly prostrating force. Finally, for a poet, there is the irresistible impulse to bring words to bear on it. This entails accepting language's ruthless insistence on speaking it as it really is – of speaking of it not only as 'loss' but as 'disaster'.

'To me alone there came a thought of grief,' wrote William Wordsworth, but 'A timely utterance gave that thought relief/ And I again am strong.' The poems in this collection all aspire to be 'timely utterances', utterances that relieve, however briefly, the unbearable pressure of loss by giving verbal vent to it. But each and every one is also a 'laboratory of the spirit,' because we are all most searchingly 'tried,' our 'mettle' never more sorely tested, than when we struggle to come to terms with some dreadful deprivation.

But though they are rooted in grief, elegies are never direct verbal transcriptions of the experience of loss.

As Helen Vendler has perceptively but also provocatively written, 'The great effort of will required to convert grief into something that can legitimately be called not wailing or mourning or bleating but song is ... the effort required to rise from childhood to adulthood.' Elegies are what poets artfully manage to fashion out of their experience of grief. They are what they have succeeded in making of their experience – 'making' in both senses of that phrase.

In form, the traditional elegy, to which many of the poems included here approximate, follows a trajectory that traces the different stages of loss. Beginning by giving full, sometimes almost unbridled, expression to the pain, it aspires to move towards some kind of resolution that involves placing the experience in some sort of consolingly meaningful context. So, for example, a Christian elegy such as Milton's 'Lycidas' ends with the assurance that the subject of the poem is not really dead; rather, he has been transfigured and guaranteed life eternal. Whereas the 'pagan' Whitman ends his elegy for Abraham Lincoln by envisaging the fallen hero as guaranteed a different kind of immortality in the burgeoning human and physical landscape of a democratic America, for which he has sacrificed his life.

Several animals capable of forming strong bonding relationships (elephants, wolves, apes and goats) are thought to exhibit signs of grief. The human animal is no exception. As W. B. Yeats once memorably wrote, 'Man is in love and loves what vanishes./ What more is there to say?' The earliest evidence of human mourning has been dated back to Stone Age Africa, some 78,000 years ago, although evidence of a funeral has been detected even earlier. As for poems of mourning, one of the first seems to be that of Odysseus for his faithful dog Argos, in Homer's *The Odyssey*, composed some seven hundred years before Christ. The earliest poem in this collection dates back to the fifteenth century. It provides further confirmation that the experience of grief has been a human constant down the ages and is not a modern phenomenon.

'It is a fearful thing to love what Death can touch,' wrote the medieval Jewish poet Yehuda Halevi. Most of the poems in this collection are testimony to the fearfulness of all human lives in which love plays a central part.

There is one exception, however. That is a poem about the imagined loss of a language – the Welsh language. It is included here to emphasise the background of threat against which all the contemporary Welsh-language poets of Wales have inescapably to work, and to acknowledge the preciousness of their fidelity to a language that has been a core part of the identity of the Welsh people for almost two thousand years.

M. Wynn Thomas

No Toying With Death

Some scholars had argued until fairly recently that the loss of a child was such a common experience in the Middle Ages that parents had felt very little pain. But over the past few decades that theory has been comprehensively abandoned. A poem such as this heart-wrenching one by Lewys Glyn Cothi conclusively gives the lie to it.

It dates from the fifteenth century, a period when the catastrophic devastation caused in the previous century by the Black Death had made people newly aware of the precious frailty of lives both young and old. The later Great Plague also made fathers aware of their crucial responsibilities to sustain and defend their families.

And in this poem Lewys Glyn Cothi is very much the piteously grieving father. Lewys identifies himself as such in the second line, as if he were impelled by guilt to accuse himself of a failure to protect his little boy. Shortly afterwards he names him, adding 'Y Glyn' to the name Siôn and thus highlighting the fact that the 'natural' line of succession from father to son has been broken. From then on, he repeats the name as if helplessly, hopelessly impelled to continue. The little boy is named four times during the course of a short poem.

LEWYS GLYN COTHI (1420–89)

Marwnad Siôn y Glyn

detholiad

Un mab oedd degan i mi;
Dwynwen! Gwae'i dad o'i eni!
Gwae a edid, o gudab,
I boeni mwy heb un mab!
Fy nwy ais, farw fy nisyn,
Y sy'n glaf am Siôn y Glyn.
Udo fyth yr ydwyf fi
Am benáig mabinogi.

Afal pêr ac aderyn
A garai'r gwas, a gro gwyn;
Bwa o flaen y ddraenen,
Cleddau digon brau o bren.
Ofni'r bib, ofni'r bwbach,
Ymbil â'i fam am bêl fach.
Canu i bawb acen o'i ben,
Canu 'ŵo' er cneuen.
Gwneuthur moethau, gwenieithio,
Sorri wrthyf fi wnâi fo,
A chymod er ysglodyn
Ac er dis a garai'r dyn.

Och nad Siôn, fab gwirion gwâr,
Sy'n ail oes i Sain Lasar!
Beuno a droes iddo saith
Nefolion yn fyw eilwaith;
Gwae eilwaith, fy ngwir galon,
Nad oes wyth rhwng enaid Siôn.

O Fair, gwae fi o'i orwedd!
A gwae fy ais gau ei fedd!
Yngo y saif angau Siôn
Yn ddeufrath yn y ddwyfron:
Fy mab, fy muarth baban,
Fy mron, fy nghalon, fy nghân,
Fy mryd cyn fy marw ydoedd,
Fy mardd doeth, fy mreuddwyd oedd;
Fy nhegan oedd, fy nghannwyll,
Fy enaid teg, fy un twyll,
Fy nghyw yn dysgu fy nghân,
Fy nghae Esyllt, fy nghusan,
Fy nerth, gwae fi yn ei ôl!
Fy ehedydd, fy hudol,
Fy serch, fy mwa, fy saeth,
F'ymbiliwr, fy mabolaeth.

LEWYS GLYN COTHI (1420–89);

MY TRANSLATION

Elegy for Siôn y Glyn

a selection

One son was my toy;
Alas, Saint Dwynwen, that he was born!
Woe to doting parent, bereft,
Forever grieving his one son!
My heart, robbed of its darling,
Breaks for Siôn y Glyn.
Forever I mourn
The lost lord of boyhood adventure.

The lad loved a sweet apple.
A bird and white pebbles;
A bow bent from thorn,
Brittle swords of wood;
Afraid of piping, and of bogeys,
Begging his mother for a small ball;
Serenading all winningly,
Hot on a nut's trail;
Coyly charming and cajoling,
Cross when crossed,
Pacified by a bit of wood
And the dice he so loved.

Oh that Siôn, lovely gentle lad,
Were another Saint Lazarus!
St Beuno restored to life
Seven who'd passed over;
Oh that Siôn weren't eighth.

Virgin Mother, he's been felled!
My breast aches at closed grave!
Dead Siôn's embedded there
Double stab to my chest:
My son, my little sparkler,
My bosom, my heart, my song,
My hope before I die,
My wise poet, my dream;
My plaything, my candle,
My fair soul, my charmer,
My chick learning my song,
My Iseult's coronal, my kisses,
My strength, fatally sapped!
My lark, my wizard,
My passion, my bow, my arrow,
My little beggar, my youth.

Lewys Glyn Cothi – a name that identifies him as a native of the Llanybydder area in Cardiganshire – was one of the major Welsh poets of the late Medieval period. Like all such poets, he tramped the length and breadth of Wales visiting wealthy houses and Cistercian abbeys. They provided him with food and shelter in return for the gossip he brought and the poems he sang. He probably had some experience as a soldier supporting the Lancastrian cause in the Wars of the Roses, and may also have spent periods as an outlaw on the run. But as this poem shows, he was also naturally something of a home bird, devoted to his family – some of his poems demonstrate a capacity for affection in an age when greater emphasis was beginning to be placed on sensibility.

His little son died at the age of five, and the highly individuated picture of him painted in the most enchanting passage of this poem vividly portrays a little boy's sulks, fears, tantrums and winning ways. Lewys was clearly entranced by them all. Later in the poem, he bestows epithets on the boy as he might shower kisses, invoking him as his son, his skylark, his magician, his love, his bow, his arrow, his very youth. The phrases tumble out willy nilly, and the emphasis throughout is on the little

one's infectious vivacity. It is implicitly connected with the energy of creativity, so that his death seems to have sapped Lewys's strength as a poet. He also calls him 'fy mardd doeth'/'my wise poet' and 'fy nghyw yn dysgu fy nghân'/ 'my chick learning my song' – clearly implying that Siôn had begun to be instructed in the complex arts of poetry, and so been destined to succeed his father one day. In Welsh, the 'buarth baban', here translated as 'sparkler', refers to the practice of twirling a burning brand to entrance a little child. As for the reference to 'Iseult's coronal', Lewys seems to be poignantly imagining the adornment in love his child might have been in manhood. And although it is thus a heavily male-centred poem, it does offer a brief glimpse of the boy's mother as her little son begs her to give him a ball.

Also notable is that the elegy makes no effort to find consolation in religious belief. Lewys bleakly recognises that the age of miracles (St Lazarus; St Beuno) is long over and with it any hope for the restoration of the dead to life. So the poem ends with Lewys bidding a final, irrevocable farewell to his son. In its full version it concludes, to devastating effect, by naming him one last time: 'Siôn fy mab!'/ 'my son Siôn!'

A Young Moon Entombed

William Wordsworth once famously wrote of being surprised by joy. But one can also be surprised by grief. This early nineteenth-century poem perfectly captures the experience of being stunned, bewildered by totally unexpected sorrow. The last two lines in particular convey the sensation of unreality, or perhaps of surreal displacement, that is such a familiar part of the human response to sudden, totally unanticipated, loss. The final image of a young moon buried beneath the ground registers the violent upending of the familiar cosmos of personal experience, as well as of the 'natural' order of things.

ROBERT AP GWILYM DDU (1777–1850)

Awdl Goffa am ei Ferch

detholiad

Och gur! pwy fesur pa faint
Yw 'nghwyn mewn ing a henaint?
At bwy trof yn fy ngofid
A chael lle i ochel llid?

Angau arfog, miniog, mawr,
Ar ei gadfarch ergydfawr,
Wele yma carlamodd,
A'i rym ar egni a rôdd.
Torrodd i lawr drwy fawr feth
Ein diddig unig eneth,
A mynnodd hwnt o'n mynwes
Enaid a llygaid ein lles …

Dwfn guddiwyd, ataliwyd hi,
Y man na welwyf mohoni.
Llwch y llawr, yn awr, er neb,
Sy heno dros ei hwyneb.
Nid oes wên i'w rhieni
Ar ei hôl, er nas gŵyr hi.

Ymholais, crwydrais mewn cri; – och alar!
  Hir chwiliais amdani;
 Chwilio'r celloedd oedd eiddi,
 A chwilio heb ei chael hi …

Och arw sôn, ni cheir seinio – un mesur
  Na musig piano;
 Mae'r gerdd annwyl yn wylo,
 A'r llaw wen dan grawen gro.

Ochenaid uwch ei hannedd – a roesom;
  Mae'n resyn ei gorwedd;
 Lloer ifanc mewn lle rhyfedd,
 Gwely di-barch, gwaelod bedd …

ROBERT AP GWILYM DDU (1777–1850);

MY TRANSLATION

Elegy for his Daughter

a selection

The pain, who'll measure
I ask in age and anguish?
Where find – in my loss –
Respite from bitter anger?

Armed death – fierce, mighty –
Astride powerful war-steed,
Galloped towards me.
Full force his blow
Scythed our darling child,
Our only, blithe, girl
Torn from our breast,
Soul and quick of our being …

Deep-hidden, arrested,
Detained beyond ken.
Earth's crust, despite all,
Tonight covers her face.
No smile for her parents –
though she knows not –
now she's gone.

I enquired, wandered
Bereft – oh! grief! –
Searched long for her;
Scoured every room,
Searched without finding …

Song's stilled, music silent,
Piano dumb;
Poem weeps,
White hand 'neath pebbly crust.

One sigh above her dwelling
We heaved in our regret:
Crescent moon in strange location,
Rude, crude bed, grave's pit …

Robert ap Gwilym Ddu, whose baptismal name was Robert Williams, lost his darling daughter Jane when she was just seventeen. He was a modestly prosperous farmer in the vicinity of Llanystumdwy. It is a village just down the road from Cricieth, on the Llŷn Peninsula, now best known as first home and then final resting place of David Lloyd George. When young, Robert had received local training in the traditional strict metres, but had then departed from convention by opting not to adopt the high style of conventional *barddas* or to address its elevated subjects. He preferred to produce a more colloquial poetry suited to recording the daily life of his period.

But it is nevertheless his high skill in the strict metres that enabled him to fashion this marvellous elegy, whose terse, clipped, lapidary style is perfect for conveying the sense of being helplessly, hopelessly, imprisoned by loss. There is a sense of verbal confinement corresponding both to Jane's final and eternal confinement under ground and to Robert ap Gwilym Ddu's frustration at being unable to rid himself of his bitterness, anger and overwhelming sorrow by adequately venting it in language. The silence, the stillness and the emptiness he images are the attributes

of the vacuum left in his existence now that all that mattered to him in life has been sucked out of it.

Rather unusual, and correspondingly affecting, is the movement in the poem from the singular to the plural, as he comes to acknowledge that the loss has been his wife's every bit as much as his. And so they unite in a moment of mute, impotent solidarity, over their young daughter's final resting place.

He was a deeply devout man, author of a powerful hymn, still popular with congregations today, wondering at the salvation that continued mysteriously to flow from the blood shed on Calvary. Indeed the last section of his elegy, which is omitted here, is devoted to an attempt to reconcile his loss to his faith. The elegy thus follows the classic pattern – raw expression of pain and anger (for a Christian, there is startling frankness in that opening confession of a feeling of resentment), gradually moderating and modulating into acceptance, on whatever terms the mourner finds comfort in accepting. In the case of a traditional Christian believer, that will of course take the form of trust in the Almighty. In Robert ap Gwilym Ddu's case, the fact that the young girl also firmly believed in eternal life enables him, in the poem's final sections, to

find a consoling common ground between himself and his dead daughter.

And so, the concluding lines include a memorable couplet of calm assurance, in which Robert ap Gwilym Ddu – now reverting once more to the first-person singular – touchingly looks forward to 'Cael tragwyddol gydfoli/ Mewn eilfyd hyfryd â hi': to an eternal afterlife of singing everlasting praise in her company. It's as if the body warmth of loving physical contact were transposed to an ethereal key in an image of close, intimate, vocal harmony. The musical image picks up on the earlier memory of his beloved daughter playing the piano, and of the literally deathly silence following her passing. Also powerful is his description of her grave as a crude 'gwely di-barch', which is an 'unmannerly' bed, or a discourteous bed. And the word is all the more effective, because from beginning to end the elegy is full of an unaffected dignity of expression. In style, form, timbre and bearing it conveys a courtesy of utterance even though the pent-up rage and anguish of the sufferer is unmistakeable.

A Black Trench of Loss

Hedd Wyn: thirty years ago the name was up in lights in Hollywood. A Welsh film of that name had been nominated for an Oscar in the best foreign film category. The usual razzmatazz duly followed. In Wales excitement steadily mounted – and was shortly extinguished. It did not win. And had it done so, there would have been something at once exhilarating and faintly disquieting about its success. The film, much of which featured the Welsh language, told the story of a young poet, from Trawsfynydd in rural Gwynedd, who was condemned to die in a distant land in the obscene swampland of the trenches. To him, a Welsh-speaking Christian pacifist, W. B. Yeats's famous lines about an Irish airman shot down over wartime France could be appropriately applied:

> Those that I fight I do not hate
> Those that I guard I do not love;
> My country is Kiltartan Cross,
> My countrymen Kiltartan's poor,
> No likely end could bring them loss
> Or leave them happier than before.

As the film made clear, the first language of Hedd Wyn (real name Ellis Humphrey Evans) was Welsh. English was to him a foreign language, and the war of the English a foreign war. And from the very beginning his death, its memorable circumstances and consequences, entered the realm of Welsh legend.

Ten years later after Hedd Wyn's death at the age of thirty in 1917, R. Williams Parry, one of the most lavishly gifted of major Welsh-language poets, and himself a native of that region of north-west Wales to which Hedd Wyn belonged, wrote an elegy for him that was immediately recognised as a classic.

R. WILLIAMS PARRY (1884–1956)

Hedd Wyn

Y bardd trwm dan bridd tramor, – y dwylaw
  Na ddidolir rhagor:
 Y llygaid dwys dan ddwys ddôr,
 Y llygaid na all agor.

Wedi ei fyw y mae dy fywyd, – dy rawd
  Wedi ei rhedeg hefyd;
 Daeth awr i fynd i'th weryd,
 A daeth i ben deithio byd.

Tyner yw'r lleuad heno – tros fawnog
  Trawsfynydd yn dringo;
 Tithau'n drist a than dy ro
 Ger y ffos ddu'n gorffwyso.

Trawsfynydd! Tros ei feini – trafaeliaist
  Ar foelydd Eryri;
 Troedio wnest ei rhedyn hi,
 Hunaist ymhell ohoni.

R. WILLIAMS PARRY (1884–1956);

MY TRANSLATION

Hedd Wyn

Sad poet 'neath foreign sod – hands
    Never again unfolded:
  Keen sight 'neath thick door,
  Eyes never to be opened.

Lived your life – your course
    Fully run;
  Time to be earthed,
  Far journeys ended.

Tender the moon tonight – o'er
    Trawsfynydd peatland climbing;
  You, grave under gravel,
  Rest near dark trench.

Trawsfynydd! its crags you clambered
    On Snowdon's bare slopes;
  Trod its green ferns,
  Slumbered far distant.

The poem is an interestingly unconventional example of that age-old genre: pastoral elegy. In that genre, the identification of the dead person as a shepherd, and all the accompanying rural paraphernalia of flora and fauna was traditionally figurative. In Hedd Wyn's case it was literal. His family's 168 acre hill farm, on the edge of Eryri, required extensive shepherding. In order to help there, he had dropped out of education at the age of 14, and had then taught himself the rudiments of Welsh poetry. He had volunteered for the Front in order to spare his younger brother, who was already running the farm.

As for the *englyn* form, that is a long-established Welsh genre with its roots in the mists of antiquity. In using it, Williams Parry is therefore dignifying a young fledgling poet, by implicitly associating him with the greats of the Welsh bardic past. Rather like the Greek Epigraph, the *englyn* is an exercise in eloquent brevity. Every word seems to have been chiselled in stone, and the complex infrastructure of sounds unique to *cynghanedd* serve as the wall-ties of clipped expression. The result is a compression of meaning that has tensile strength and explosive power.

Hedd Wyn had spent his final days before enlistment composing a long poem. As a result, he outstayed his leave. So the Military Police hunted him down, seizing him as he was working in a hayfield. The poem was his entry for the Chair, the chief poetry competition at the National Eisteddfod. That year, it was held over the border in Birkenhead. And Guest of Honour was David Lloyd George, whose notorious speech in September 1914 urging the Welsh to display their vaunted valour, had so fatefully boosted recruitment in Wales.

In the climactic event, Hedd Wyn's chosen *nom de plume* was duly declared from the stage to be the winner. The trumpets sounded. The expectant crowd waited for the winner to declare himself by rising to his feet. But a deathly silence fell. Hedd Wyn had, as the organisers already knew, been killed a short time earlier, fatally wounded in the stomach at the battle of Pilckem Ridge, the opening engagement of the bloodbath known as The Battle of Passchendaele. In front of a shocked crowd the empty chair was ceremonially draped in funereal black. Carried by train to a station near the poet's home, it was there shouldered by Hedd Wyn's friends, who silently

carried it on their shoulders all the way to the remote farm. It was a scene that cried out for filmic treatment.

What Rupert Brooke is to the English, Hedd Wyn is to the Welsh. But a greater contrast could scarcely be imagined between two poets who shared the same grim fate. Rupert Brooke was bellicose and jingoistic; Hedd Wyn a pacifist who viewed the war as a moral obscenity. The title of his prize-winning poem was 'Yr Arwr', 'The Hero.' But it did not praise military prowess and has been forgotten. What has been remembered are other lines by Hedd Wyn – his very name means 'Blessed Peace'. And these powerful lines are a fitting epitaph for Hedd Wyn himself:

Gwae fi fy myw mewn oes mor ddreng,
A Duw ar drai ar orwel pell;
O'i ôl mae dyn, yn deyrn a gwreng,
Yn codi ei awdurdod hell.
...
Mae'r hen delynau genid gynt
Ynghrog ar gangau'r helyg draw,
A gwaedd y bechgyn lond y gwynt,
A'u gwaed yn gymysg efo'r glaw.

Why must I live in this grim age,
When, to a far horizon, God
Has ebbed away, and man, with rage,
Now wields the sceptre and the rod?
...
The harps to which we sang are hung
On willow boughs, and their refrain
Drowned by the anguish of the young
Whose blood is mingled with the rain.
(trans. Alan Llwyd)

Bomb Damage

The sudden, violent death of Alun Lewis in 1944 in Burma, in ambiguous circumstances, was a great loss to poetry. His exceptional talent as a writer was just beginning to manifest itself. This poem of his is hauntingly enigmatic. But then, so was Alun Lewis himself, prey from youth onwards to what he graphically described as 'the Gestapo' who tortured his mind. Brooding and melancholic, he possessed a gently reflective personality that effortlessly attracted many to him. Inclined towards pacifism, on Socialist grounds, he nevertheless ended up reluctantly volunteering for service, and then, having been assigned an officer's rank, resolutely refused all the privileges attendant upon it – insisting, for example, on messing with the ordinary soldiers, in whose company alone he felt comfortable.

The collection of the same name as this poem was his first. Published in 1942, it included a record of the period following his enlistment. This poem is a response to the London of the blitz, when the bombing stripped walls off houses, leaving intimate interiors obscenely exposed. The concluding stanza offers us sight of a violently disordered domesticity, a voyeuristic glimpse of a private female environment that has been violated. It has about it a sensuousness that is vaguely disturbing. From the first, Lewis never shrank from the sometimes disconcerting complexity of human response even to scenes of catastrophe. There is a sexual frisson to that image of a startled beauty. And it is there again in that electrifying juxtaposition of blue necklace and charred chair.

ALUN LEWIS (1915–44)

Raiders' Dawn

Softly the civilized
Centuries fall,
Paper on paper,
Peter on Paul.

And lovers waking
From the night –
Eternity's masters,
Slaves of Time –
Recognize only
The drifting white
Fall of small faces
In pits of lime.

Blue necklace left
On a charred chair
Tells that Beauty
Was startled there.

The opening stanza reads like a seductively sinister nursery rhyme which also has to it something of the insinuating lilt of a lullaby. In its 'softness' it conveys the terrible ease with which civilisation and all its strenuously achieved civilities just melts soundlessly away in the eruptive presence of savage barbarism. Lewis knew his T. S. Eliot well, and there could be an oblique reference in the mention of Peter and Paul to Eliot's celebrated image of the falling towers of great cities, since Lewis may have had in mind the churches of St Peter's in Rome and St Paul's in London. But equally well, the reference could be to the Saints themselves, two of the main pillars of Christianity.

As for the reference to lovers, it no doubt arose from his memories of his own snatched night of wedded bliss. He and Gweno Ellis married on impulse at Gloucester Registry Office in July 1941. En route there he stole a spray of roses overhanging a wall to provide her with a bouquet. The next day he headed back to his Officers' Training Camp. Later he was to recall 'Mouth on mouth, spirit and flesh at one,/ We fused the eternal stars with the touch of time./ And our lips were salt and swollen with tears.'

And the phantasmagoric air of the whole nightmare poem is wonderfully enhanced by that extraordinary vision of 'small faces/ In pits of lime.' Lime, the great soft, caustic solvent of human flesh. It conveys a sense of universal dissolution occurring in a seductively soft way, as if the will to resist had been fatally undermined. The poem as a whole is a remarkable memorial to the innumerable, anonymous losses of wartime. Losses inhumanly measured in the mass and by the ton.

Lewis himself was lost to literature in Burma (where the British were repelling a Japanese offensive) on the morning of Sunday, 5 March 1944. After shaving and washing, he'd left for the latrines; a shot was heard; Lewis was found, revolver in hand, lying mortally wounded from a bullet in the right temple. He was twenty-eight. Back home, Gweno was proofreading the last of his two poetry collections, *Ha! Ha! Among the Trumpets.* A hastily convened military enquiry declared his to have been an accidental death. All his comrades were certain that he had taken his own life. In his poem 'Post-Script: for Gweno' he had movingly written:

> If I should go away,
> Beloved, do not say
> 'He has forgotten me'.
> For you abide
> A singing rib within my dreaming side;
> You always stay.

Funeral Strange

Women have until recently been reticent on the subject of miscarriage. They have proved reluctant to speak of this painful, and uniquely female, experience of loss, in part because they have instinctively realised that men tend to have little comprehension or sympathy with it. The clunky modern label for it is 'disenfranchised mourning'; a mourning that society at large does not recognise. One of the brave souls who did break that taboo of silence as long as half a century ago was Menna Elfyn. She was then a young poet starting out on what has proved to be an illustrious career which has earned her international recognition. In so doing, she risked the hostility of men, and that hostility was not slow in coming. She was roundly condemned by the male cultural establishment of the day in Wales for her indelicacy. Miscarriage, they loftily opined, was no fit subject for poetry.

But Menna Elfyn was well used to controversy. In her youth, she had been a prominent member of Cymdeithas yr Iaith Gymraeg, the young generation's movement to establish full legal recognition for the Welsh language. For her part in the pulling down of monolingual English road signs she served a brief period in prison. Courage therefore was already her middle name. And the following poem remains electrifying because of the unflinching boldness with which she finds daring expression for her harrowing experience of loss. Throughout her life Menna Elfyn has been an impassioned campaigner against every form of racial discrimination, as for the rights of minority cultures and subordinated peoples worldwide.

MENNA ELFYN (1951–)

Angladd

'Chest ti ddim arwyl,
un parchus cefn-gwlad;
dim ond dy daflu'n fflwcsyn
i boethder fflamau
megis papur newydd ddoe –
heddiw'n ddiwerth; –
dy arch oedd bag plastig
fel y 'lasog a dryloywa
o berfedd ffowlyn.
'Chanodd neb emyn
na heulio gweddi –
'chest ti mo'th ganmol,
na'th gofleidio –
ond yn nwrn y doctor da.

Minnau 'fatraf gân
i'r angladd unigol,
ger tramwyfa prysur salwch,
uwch goleuadau treisiol ysbyty:
mynegaf ddwyster y myfyr olaf
cyn gadael dy farwnad i fynd.

MENNA ELFYN (1951–)

Funeral

No funeral you had, no
respectable burial in the country –
only a scrap of rubbish
for the incinerator
like yesterday's news –
today it's useless.
Your coffin was a see-through gizzard
From a chicken's gut.
No one sang a hymn
or spread prayers over you.
You had no praise
No one hugged you
except the good doctor in his fist.

But I, I shall unwrap a song
for that solitary exequy
in the busy toing and froing of sickness
over the hospital's aggressive lights:
I'll reach to the very last solemn thought
before I'll let go my elegy for you.

Menna Elfyn admitted that she had no liking for the fifteen-hundred-year-old Welsh tradition of elegy. For her, it was a species of the praise poetry she abhorred, because it seemed so creepily ingratiating. A veritable Uriah Heep of a genre. And part of the strength of this poem is that it is such a radically different elegy that, in the context of the Welsh elegiac tradition, it seems almost like an anti-elegy. It is certainly an intentionally 'alternative' one. So when she announces defiantly that she will 'unwrap her song', it is with a hint of anger in her voice that no words had ever previously been spared to commemorate those innumerable tiny embryonic human beings over the long centuries who were lost before ever they were even born. That lacerating anger is felt when she discloses the lack of human respect shown in the treatment of the foetus as nothing but a piece of rubbish fit only to be carelessly discarded.

It is against the background of this shocking disrespect that she insists on terming her poem an 'exequy' – that rather posh word for funeral ceremonies and processions is deliberately introduced to inject a degree of ritualistic

gravity and grandeur into the poem, appropriate to the memorialising of any human experience of loss. Exequies are not the preserve of the rich and the powerful and the prominent. The shift to formal poetic syntax and vocabulary in that last stanza ('But I, I shall unwrap a song') marks the point at which Elfyn directly claims from the male elegists the right to honour her own dead, just as the lines that follow mark the point where she snatches her baby back, in imagination, from the depersonalising milieu of the heavily masculinised world of modern medicine. These verbal gestures are the counter-attack of one who feels, as woman and as poet, that her utterance, like her uterus, has been contemptuously disregarded.

And what moves her to such aggression is a mother's instinct to protect her helpless offspring. These lines are a protective, belated verbal embrace, which is also the soft shawl of a winding-sheet. The words are lapped gently around the foetus in order to ensure, and secure, a safe place for it within the human world. And the concluding phrases ('I'll reach to the very last solemn thought') contain within them a multitude of commitments: to make sure

that last thoughts of the departed baby are lasting ones; to insist on the intensity of such an undervalued loss; to discover in this supposedly 'insignificant' instance the type of *all* mourning and, indeed, the wrenching evidence of our own mortality. These meanings are even more hauntingly present in the original Welsh, the syntax of which allows the last line to be understood to mean 'before I let go my elegy in order to go' ('cyn gadael dy farwnad i fynd'). The unspoken purpose of every elegy is, after all, to fit us again, but in a new way, for life.

Even as Menna Elfyn struggles, then, to fashion elegy anew in an effort to find appropriate forms of expression for a uniquely female experience, she clearly exposes those normally hidden ingredients of grieving that psychoanalysts have long insisted constitute the true profile of every experience of loss, regardless of gender. Resentment, anger, a mingled sense of guilt and personal betrayal – these emotions so quickly sublimated into sadness in conventional elegiac practice become nakedly apparent under circumstances that so obviously licence such a reaction.

She is aware from the very beginning that there is no pattern of language she can follow when setting out to compose her unique elegy. She has to find words adequate to the experience for the very first time in Welsh tradition. That she succeeds in doing so is a real achievement for a woman poet from Wales. Particularly affecting is the moment when she registers desolately that the little one was denied even the comfort of a maternal hug, just as she, a mourning mother, had been denied even the fleeting consolation of holding her baby close.

Haunted Landscape

The Abergwesyn Pass. The road over it is one of the loneliest and most atmospheric in Wales, as it wends its way through the bare upland area separating Tregaron from Llanwrtyd. The whole region is replete with history and legend. The little town of Tregaron, buried deep in the very heart of mid-Wales, was for centuries the jumping-off point for the drovers, who used to drive their flocks over the Pass to distant markets in London and the English Midlands. On the square stands a monument to Henry Richard, the renowned late- nineteenth-century 'Apostle of Peace.' He devoted his life as an MP to working for the cause of international harmony. His achievements were such that he is regarded as one of those who laid the foundations first for the League of Nations and then for the United Nations.

Where the Pass begins to descend towards Llanwrtyd Wells the traveller passes through the realm that was until recently the last refuge of the red kite, and the supposed haunts of the legendary Twm Siôn Catti, a Welsh folk hero beloved for robbing the rich to give to the poor.

Along the way a road branches off to Soar y Mynydd, the little, plain, isolated Nonconformist chapel, now rarely used, that once served a scattered community of farmers and shepherds. For R. S. Thomas it was one of the most sacred spots in the whole of Wales. It was there that he felt he'd come closest to the very soul of the Welsh people.

It was to this fascinating area that Ruth Bidgood, a native of Port Talbot with a lifetime of service as a civil servant, chose to retire. And it was here that she first began to write poems when already into her sixties. As they grew in number, they began to take the form of a kind of cultural cartography, a poetic mapping of an area whose once-flourishing communities had steadily declined throughout the twentieth century, until all that was left was lonely remains and fading memories. Her best poems are therefore elegies for a lost community, and its richly idiomatic Welsh-language dialect. The following is one of her most resonantly plangent.

RUTH BIDGOOD (1922–2022)

All Souls'

Shutting my gate, I walk away
from the small glow of my banked fire
into a black All Souls'. Presently
the sky slides back across the void
like a grey film. Then the hedges
are present, and the trees, which my mind
already knows, are no longer
strangers to my eyes.
The road curves. Further along,
a conversation of lights begins
from a few houses, invisible except as light,
calling to farms that higher in darkness
answer still, though each now
speaks for others that lie dumb.

Light at Tŷmawr above me, muted by trees,
is all the voice Brongwesyn has,
that once called clearly enough
into the upper valley's night.
From the hill Clyn ahead
Glangwesyn's lively shout of light
celebrates old Nant Henfron, will not let
Cenfaes and Blaennant be voiceless.
I am a latecomer, but offer
speech to the nameless, those
who are hardly a memory, those
whose words were always faint
against the deafening darkness
of remotest hills.
For them tonight when I go home
I will draw back my curtains, for them
my house shall sing with light.

In the Church calendar, the evening of All Souls' Day (November 2) is a special time, when the partition between the living and dead seems to become mysteriously thinned, to allow us intimate communication with those who have passed over. It is a Christian Festival of Lights when votive candles are lit, and in some areas placed on graves. As the daughter of an Anglican vicar, Bidgood would have grown up observing that festival, but not so the people that she here commemorates. They would all have been chapel people, and for them it was Sul y Blodau (the Sunday before Easter, Palm Sunday) that served as an All Souls' Day. There is therefore an unintended incongruity in her observing All Souls' Night on their behalf in her poem. It is evidence that not only is she a 'latecomer' to these parts, as the poem acknowledges, but also inescapably something of an outsider, desperately though she wants to identify with what remains of the upland community that has grown dear to her.

But her thoughts are not only for the dead. The poem is a celebration of the traditional solidarities and related personal and social strengths, the remnants of which she finds in the reduced communities. One of her favourite words is 'hauntings'. Hauntings aplenty there indeed are in this poem, but they are also blessings, if somewhat equivocally so. She glories in the 'conversation of lights,' as dusk falls over this sparsely populated upland landscape. Not only is every farmhouse, remote and isolated though it seems, sending out touchingly fragile filaments of fellow-feeling – what Walt Whitman had called 'retrievals out of the night' – but those lights seem to her to be anxious to speak 'for others that lie dumb.'

Bidgood was a monoglot English speaker. She was very aware that when she wrote poems mourning the passing of a culturally sophisticated Welsh-language community, she did so in the very language that had contributed largely to its displacement and eventual disappearance. Her guilt was further complicated by personal experience; she had herself been deprived of the Welsh language, so that her elegies became poems of mourning for what she had herself lost. There is therefore a particular poignancy to the very names of the farms she liturgically invokes – 'Tŷmawr', 'Brongwesyn', 'Glangwesyn', 'Nant Henfron', Cenfaes', 'Blaennant' – because the Welsh language of which they are composed is at even greater risk of obliteration than are the farms themselves. To register this is to apprehend a new dimension of meaning in every use she makes of words such as 'conversation', 'voice', 'speech' and so on.

But at its end, the poem opens out into the universal. The darkness of All Souls' Night, engulfing a human life whose faint presence remains only in those frail lights, brings home to her (in more than one sense) the immensity of the non-human universe. The ending is therefore a kind of prayer for all humanity, and a prayer *to* humanity, that it cherish the common bonds that constitute its only strength.

The Massacre of the Innocents

On the morning of 21 October 1966, the Taff Valley was shrouded in autumn mist. It was drizzling. And it had rained solidly throughout the previous week. But the little children at Pantglas Junior School were excited, because it was the last day before the holidays. There was a scuffle around the Wendy House, since too many children wanted to play in it. They had just settled at their desks – one little girl beginning to write a story about a snowman – when they heard a noise 'like an aeroplane coming in to land.' The recently appointed deputy headmaster, David Beynon, heard it too. He had little time to act, but he braced himself against a blackboard and called the nearest children to join him.

In the immediate aftermath of the disaster, hundreds of miners from a very wide area rushed to the rescue. Many had no tools and had to work with their bare hands. Every so often a whistle would sound as they were clearing the slurry, and they would stop digging and fall silent. Someone had been detected. Yvonne Price, a young police officer who rushed to the scene, recalled how they were soon 'bringing out the dead children. One of the miners

passing them through on the stretchers looked at one child and passed him on. And he just looked at me and said "That was my child". And he just carried on working.' After 11.00 no further survivors were found. When the appalling black mountain of slurry – 33 feet deep in some classrooms – was finally cleared, David Beynon was found with five of the children wrapped in his arms. 109 of his pupils were dead, as were 5 of his colleagues. He had been an outstanding footballer and rugby player, and at school in Merthyr had been a friend of Leslie Norris, who went on to be a prominent poet.

The response of the Labour government to the disaster was a disgrace. At the coroner's inquest into the deaths, one grieving father called out in protest at the little bodies being described as victims of an accident, 'No, sir – buried alive by the National Coal Board.' The National Coal Bard had been warned innumerable times that the spoil tip represented an imminent hazard. But the NCB 'spin-doctored' its way out of trouble, and no-one was ever charged. The report of the public enquiry concluded 'that the Aberfan disaster could and should have been prevented.'

Yet those who had lost their children were expected to pay, from the money that had flowed into their appeal fund from all over the world, for the removal of what remained of the killer Tip No. 7. The event was the grimmest imaginable epilogue to the catalogue of disasters that had punctuated the history of the coal mining industry in south Wales. A catastrophic explosion at nearby Senghenydd Colliery on 14 October 1913 had claimed the lives of 439 miners.

The Aberfan disaster was, and remains, literally unspeakable. 'Where I live,' reported one survivor all of fifty years later, 'there are children playing nearby and it kind of freaks me out.' But even ordinary people nevertheless felt impelled to try to find a language that would ensure it would be remembered. Fifty years later, one of the survivors, who had never previously said a word about what happened, 'got a piece of paper and a pen and I just let it come out. I just found it easier to do it in verse.' And understandably, that urge to relieve the pain by capturing it in language was felt just as acutely by Leslie Norris.

LESLIE NORRIS (1921–2006)

Elegy for David Beynon

David, we must have looked comic, sitting
there at the next desks; your legs stretched
half-way down the classroom, while
my feet hung a free inch above

the floor. I remember, too, down
at The Gwynne's Field, at the side
of the little Taff, dancing with
laughing fury as you caught

effortlessly at the line-out, sliding
the ball over my head direct to
the outside-half. That was Cyril
Theophilus, who died in his quiet

so long ago that only I, perhaps,
remember he'd hold the ball one-handed
on his thin stomach as he turned
to run. Even there you were careful

to miss us with your scattering
knees as you bumped through
for yet another try. Buffeted
we were, but cheered too by our

unhurt presumption in believing
we could ever have pulled you down.
I think those children, those who died
under your arms in the crushed school,

would understand that I make this
your elegy. I know the face you had,
have walked with you enough mornings
under the fallen leaves. Theirs is

the great anonymous tragedy one word
will summarise. Aberfan, I write it
for them here, knowing we've paid to it
our shabby pence, and now it can be stored

with whatever names there are where
children end their briefest pilgrimage.
I cannot find words for you, David. These
are too long, too many; and not enough.

This is a subdued poem, of muted expression. As if language itself were stunned by the story it has been asked to tell. Since David Beynon's life ended in a classroom, it is appropriate that the elegy begins in a classroom. Even there, as a schoolboy, Beynon had stood out for his size and his physical prowess. But equally important, it establishes at the outset what a caring and gentle giant he was, even at that early age. The passing mention of the premature passing of another school friend in Cyril Theophilus becomes a premonition of what is to come.

At the centre of the poem, Norris seeks sanction for the temerity of his elegy from the children whom Beynon had taught and tried to save. His poem is not only fashioned to commemorate them and his friend, but presented as their gesture of thanks for what their

teacher had attempted to do for them. Norris seems to be speaking on behalf of the dead littles ones who are powerless to speak for themselves. Throughout, he is acutely conscious that his is a precariously justifiable undertaking; that in daring to write on this subject he is breaking a moral taboo; violating the sacred silence that would seem to be the only appropriate response to the tragedy of Aberfan. So his elegy ends with a nexus of paradoxes, in which words are simultaneously seen as unnecessary, superfluous yet essential. It is an elegy that at once affirms its verbal 'office' and undermines it. And its simplicity is in a way a studied one, as if Norris were striving to demonstrate sincerity through the parade of artlessness. But all-in-all it succeeds in being a memorably appropriate utterance, both personal and public.

A Grim Sir Galahad

The Falklands War. Or was it the Malvinas War? Britain's nobly selfless and heroically risky expedition to uphold international law, or the vainglorious gasp of a moribund British Empire? And the vast cheering, flag-waving crowds at Southampton docks. Were they proud patriots all? Or were they in the grip of a bellicose jingoism occasioned by war fever? Public opinion on such matters was, and is, deeply divided.

But, as the following elegy makes clear, Tony Conran, one of the most original and consequential of the poets of post-war Wales, had no doubt. For him, the involvement of Welsh soldiers seemed tragically consistent with the long history of a colonised Wales. Conran was acutely aware that serving in the ranks of the 'enemy' were the descendants of the nineteenth-century Welsh settlers to Patagonia, who had emigrated there to escape the destructive oppressiveness of English politics and culture. So he produced an echo-chamber of a poem, one that throughout demonstrated its awareness of being the latest example of an elegising tradition as old as that of Welsh poetry itself.

TONY CONRAN (1931–2013)

Elegy for the Welsh dead, in the Falkland Islands, 1982

Gwŷr a aeth Gatraeth oedd ffraeth eu llu.
Glasfedd eu hancwyn, a gwenwyn fu.
Men went to Catraeth, keen was their company.
They were fed on fresh mead, and it proved poison.
Men went to Catraeth. The luxury liner
For three weeks feasted them.
They remembered easy ovations,
Our boys, splendid in courage.
For three weeks the albatross roads,
Passwords of dolphin and petrel,
Practised their obedience,
Where the killer whales gathered,
Where the monotonous seas yelped.
Though they went to church with their standards
Raw death has them garnished.

Men went to Catraeth. The Malvinas
Of their destiny greeted them strangely.
Instead of affection there was coldness,
Splintering iron and the icy sea,
Mud and the wind's malevolent satire.
They stood nonplussed in the bomb's indictment.

Malcolm Wigley of Connah's Quay. Did his helm
Ride high in the war-line?
Did he drink enough mead for that journey?
The desolated shores of Tegeingl,
Did they pig this steel that destroyed him?
The Dee runs silent beside empty foundries.
The way of the wind and the rain is adamant.

Clifford Elley of Pontypridd. Doubtless he feasted.
He went to Catraeth with a bold heart.
He was used to valleys. The shadow held him.
The staff and the fasces of tribunes betrayed him.
With the oil of our virtue we have anointed
His head, in the presence of foes.

Phillip Sweet of Cwmbach. Was he shy before girls?
He exposes himself now to the hags, the glance
Of the loose-fleshed whores, the deaths
That congregate like gulls on garbage.
His sword flashed in the wastes of nightmare.

Russell Carlisle of Rhuthun. Men of the North
Mourn Rheged's son in the castellated vale.
His nodding charger neighed for the battle.
Uplifted hooves pawed at the lightning.
Now he lies down. Under the air he is dead.

Men went to Catraeth. Of the forty-three
Certainly Tony Jones of Carmarthen was brave.
What did it matter, steel in the heart?
Shrapnel is faithful now. His shroud is frost.
With the dawn went. Those forty-three,
Gentlemen all, from the streets and byways of Wales,
Dragons of Aberdare, Denbigh and Neath –
Pigment of empire, whore's honour, held them.
Forty-three at Catraeth died for our dregs.

As the opening quotation from *Y Gododdin*, the seventh-century poem about the tiny warband that was feasted for a year before being sent to face certain death, warns us, this is a poem that is richly marinated in Welsh history and 'wrinkled deep in time', to quote Shakespeare. The numerous quotations and allusions are not fanciful ornamentation. They are integral to the poem's purpose, which is to set a modern event in the context of the long, ancient history of Wales. For Conran, it is a history marked with countless examples of contemptuous foreign exploitation of the country. In the case of the Falklands War, the rapid and calamitous deindustrialisation of Wales at the hands of Margaret Thatcher had been succeeded by her callous recruitment of her doomed armed forces from among those who had become unemployed. And all in the cause of an unnecessary hubristic war which was the last example of the innumerable wars of colonial exploitation that had begun with England's conquest of Wales.

Conran's powerful stylised elegy is an act of mourning not just for the Welsh boys lost in the Falklands but for Wales itself, in its sorry modern condition. The soldiers he names with solemn ritual come from every part of the country, north and south, east and west. In the echo of the twenty-third psalm when mentioning Clifford Elley, there is an acknowledgement of the chapel heritage of Wales. In the mention of the 'way of the wind and the rain' there is a deliberate echo of Gruffudd ab yr Ynad Coch's famous elegy for the last Prince of Wales. And everywhere there is acknowledgement of the country's astonishing industrial past and its derelict present. Tegeingl is the original Welsh name of the north-east region where the huge Shotton Steelworks was situated before steel production ceased in 1980. The name came from the Deceangli, the Celtic tribe that originally lived there. As it became anglicised, so was it significantly renamed Englefield. Conran had been brought up just along the coast at Colwyn Bay.

The poem pulses with his bitter anger at the unnecessary deaths of young men 'garnished' for sacrifice. Central to it – although there is no direct mention of it (perhaps because it was so unmentionable?) – is the plight of the young Welsh soldiers on board the 'Sir Galahad' – itself a name from Arthurian legend that had been appropriated by the English. On June 8, 1982, Argentinian planes swooped in on it and its companion transport ship the 'Sir Tristram' that were anchored in Bluff Cove. 48 men on the former were killed, thirty-two of whom were from the Welsh Guards (not the 43 identified by Conran). Many of them had been burned alive. Among their number were the five commemorated in the poem.

Conran's poem is an attempt to secure an 'appropriate' memorial for these five representative figures. His is a verse laminate. It fuses together different periods of history and phases of culture. It also fuses different levels of style. 'Whore's honour,' and 'dregs' are raw expressions, contrasting with the dignified 'nodding charger' and the hooves pawing lightning. The former phrases recall Ezra Pound's memorable dismissal of World War One as a fight to save the honour of 'an old bitch gone in the teeth and a botched civilization' – his verdict on the British Empire.

But the dominant mode in Conran's elegy is the elevated style of heroic poetry. His model in all this is the distinguished London-Welsh poet and painter, David Jones, whose *In Parenthesis* is a classic poem of the First World War that foregrounds the compound, multi-regional and multi-national 'Britishness' of the troops involved.

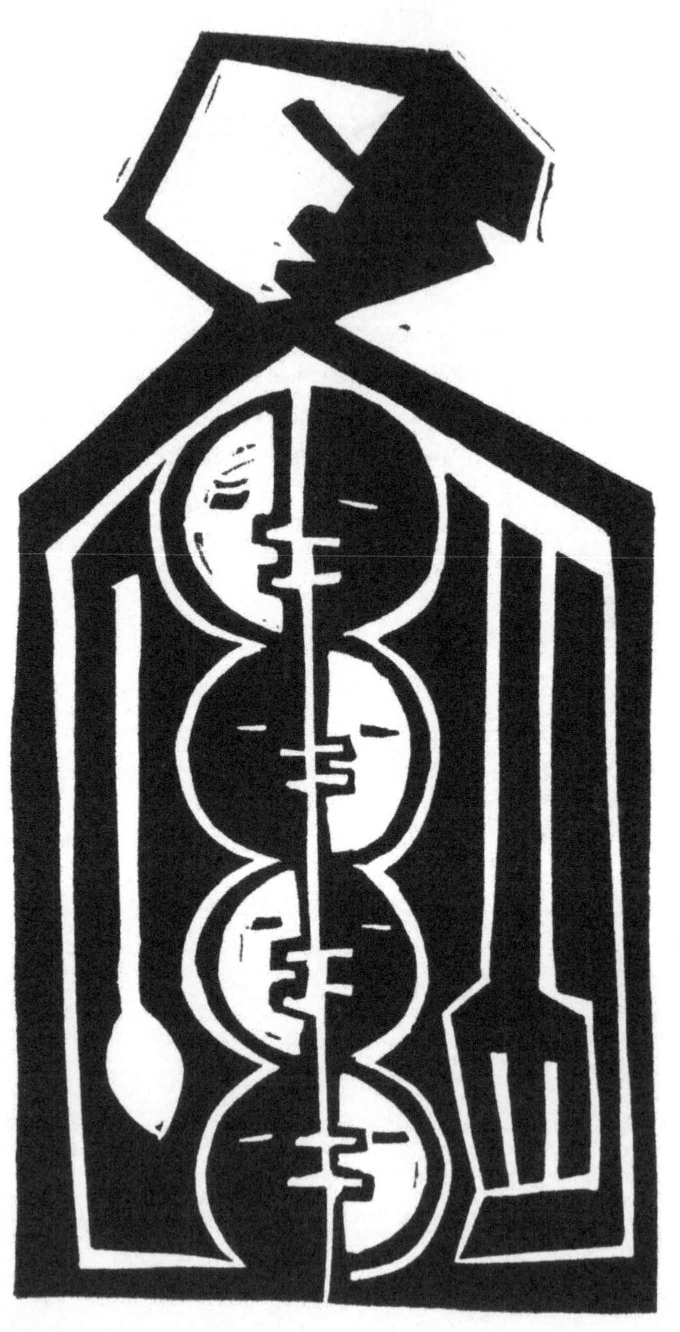

Sweeping Up the Heart

Clearing a house after a loved-one has died must surely be one of the most painful of human duties. The great American poet Emily Dickinson described it as the 'solemnest of industries' and wonderfully captured what was involved:

> The Sweeping up the Heart
> And putting Love away
> We shall not want to use again
> Until Eternity –

John Ormond was a particularly fine poet of post-war Wales as well as an internationally acclaimed documentary film-maker. He had been brought up in the village of Dunvant, on the outskirts of Swansea, where his father was a shoemaker. In his youth, he was a huge admirer of Dylan Thomas, whom he eventually met. His home was within a stone's throw of that of the prominent artist Ceri Richards. And he himself had a particular gift for art,

which evidenced itself in his films, particularly about writers and artists such as Richards, Dylan Thomas, Alun Lewis, Daniel Jones, R. S. Thomas and Vernon Watkins.

Among his beautifully fashioned poems there is a suite in which he recalls Dunvant and the life of his ancestors there, whom he affectionately acknowledges to be 'my dusty kinsfolk in the hill' – of the graveyard sloping up from the chapel on the village square. They are his 'early and lately dead,' and to them he dedicates poems of 'requiem and celebration.' The following poem is one of his most affecting, as in it he faces up to the desolating experience of bidding a final farewell to a house that is now permanently empty.

JOHN ORMOND [THOMAS] (1923–90)

After a Death

Come back to the house, I turn the key in the door,
Pull back the curtains to let out the dark,
Kindle a fire, wind up my grandfather's clock,
Then see the slug's trail on the kitchen floor.

I have inherited him with all the rest
Of whatever's here, the pictures, the jugs, the beds
Nobody sleeps in any more. Presumably, he feeds
On something here. He wouldn't come for dust.

The tables and chairs are mine, the brass trinket box,
White plates that write their O's across the dresser,
The coats and shoes in cupboards, the old letters,
The pots, the pans, the towels, the knives and forks,

The small effect of other people's lives,
And him – who wasn't mentioned in the will
Who entered from the garden once and still
From time to time inspects his territory then leaves.

A list's a list and offers me no order,
I see the silver trail, know other presences.
A death's a death. I mourn three absences,
If I wait here they'll speak when time is older.

It is a ruminative poem and a rueful one. At the beginning, the drawing back of the curtains results not in a letting in of the light, but a letting out – as if darkness has priority over light, death over life. Then there's the desolate use of that word 'inheritance', which in context does not denote valued acquisition but is prelude to a bleak inventory of loss, represented by the lifelessness of the objects numbly, routinely listed. And instead of the vitality of living speech, all that is now left of language is the row of O's that the white plates spell over the dresser – they fail even to constitute a meaningful written sentence. As for the 'small effect', that phrase bears two meanings – possessions but also consequences. Though priceless to Ormond, the ordinary lives of his dead parents were of no value or meaning once placed in the grand scale of things. Then, as if to underline this, enter the slug for a second time, the only living 'occupant' of this domestic property, whose 'territory' it has in fact become, although the will has actually bequeathed it to Ormond.

Throughout the poem, expression is low-key, emotion understated with an exaggerated care that paradoxically suggests its volcanic power. The only concession to 'weakness' comes in the first line of the last stanza, where the prostrating bewilderment of terminal loss is conveyed by that despairing remark 'A list's a list and offers me no order'. The effort made to restore a degree of normality – the kindling of a fire, the winding up of a family heirloom – is a forlorn gesture. The overwhelming feeling in the poem is one of an emptiness all the more intense for coexisting with a plenitude of objects that are now no more than relics, the husks of property that are now all that is left following the hollowing-out of the life that once gave them purpose, place and meaning. The coats and pans and so on are all utensils, and so their only purpose is to be used. Once they are not they become completely useless.

As this poem surely proves, Ormond is an underrated poet, due serious sustained attention for his quiet unshowy refinement and artistry. It was not for nothing, after all, that he was the son of a craftsman, and throughout his life he retained the deepest respect for all who possessed craft skills. In his brief elegy for his father, he pointedly remarked that 'he was no preacher.' Rather his 'working text' was an eminently practical one: 'See all dry this winter and the next.' And he concludes by simply requesting that we 'stand still. Remember his two hands, his laugh/ His craftsmanship'. In a companion poem on the same subject he acknowledges that 'from his gentle craft and his loins I woke.'

Language Death

A recurrent theme – one might say obsession – of many of the major modern Welsh-language poets of Wales is that theirs is a language on the brink of disappearing, a culture under constant duress. As Rowan Williams has rightly remarked, the result has been a remarkable body of poetry best understood not by reference to the poetry produced in dominant cultures such as those of England and the USA but through comparison with the plight of the culturally dispossessed poets in those Eastern European countries that were occupied by the Soviet Union. In a notable essay about those poets, Seamus Heaney praised their 'deviant artistic conduct … the refusal by [a] rearguard minority which exposes to the majority the abjectness of their collapse.' The comment could also be applied to the Welsh-language poets of modern Wales.

Gwyneth Lewis is one of the most talented and inventive of those poets. In 1999 she published a sequence of Welsh-language poems under the title *Y Llofrudd Iaith*. Wittily described as a 'detective novel in poetic form', it treats the imagined future death of the Welsh language as a crime, and sets out to find who has been responsible. The title is an ingenious pun. It plays on the Welsh word for 'Murder', 'Llofruddiaeth', showing that it can be split into two elements: 'Llofrudd' (Murderer) and 'Iaith' (Language). In the following poem from the sequence she imagines the linguistic confusion, the catastrophic cultural breakdown, that might be experienced by one of the last speakers of the Welsh language, as English finally extinguishes the last breath of life that remains of it in her body.

GWYNETH LEWIS (1959–)

Y Munudau Olaf

'Roedd y diwedd yn erchyll. Torrodd argae tu mewn
ac oedd gwaed ym mhobman. Allan o'i cheg
daeth rhaeadrau o eiriau *da yw dant*
i atal tafod, gogoniannau'r Tad
mewn blodau ysgarlad – *yn Abercuawg*
yd ganant gogau … roedd y gwaed yn ddu,
llawn biswail, yn ffynnon a'n synnodd ni
â'i hidiomau – *bola'n holi, ble mae 'ngheg?* –
ac o hyd yn ffrwythlon, *yes, no pwdin llo,*
ac roedd salmau'n cronni yn ei pherfeddion hi
ac yn arllwys ohoni, diarhebion, geiriau gwneud,
enwau planhigion, saith math o gnocell y coed,
gwas y neidr, criafolen, ffarwél haf
yna crawn anweddus, a thermau coll
fel *gwelltor* a *rhychor,* roedd ei chyfog fel hewl
yn arwain oddi wrthi, a byddin gref
yn gadael eu cartrefi y tu mewn i gaer
ei hanadlu, *gwŷr a aeth Gatraeth,*
Ac ar ôl yr argyfwng, doedd dim i'w wneud
ond ei gwylio hi'n marw, wrth i boer a chwys
geiriau ei gadael fel morgrug – *padell pen-glin,*
Anghydffurfiaeth, clefyd y paill,
Ac er gwaetha'n hymdrechion, erbyn y wawr
Roedd y gwaedlif yn pallu, ei gwefusau'n wyn
ac ambell ddiferyn yn tasgu. Yna dim.'

GWYNETH LEWIS (1959–)

TRANSLATION BY ROBERT MINHINNICK

The Last Minutes

'The end was horrible. A vessel burst
and there was blood everywhere. Out of her mouth
came a haemorrhage of words – *use a tooth*
to stop the tongue, glories of the Father,
In Abercuawg are cuckoos singing –
in scarlet flowers – but then the blood was black
and full of slurry – a fountain that appalled us
with its idioms – *my belly thinks my throat is cut* –
and always fertile, *yes, there's no calf pudding* –
and there were the psalms accumulated in the gut
pouring out of her, proverbs, verbs,
the names of plants, seven words for the woodpecker,
a dragonfly, the mountain ash, Michaelmas daisies,
and then the obscene gangrene of the lost terms
such as the *right ox* and *left ox,* all this retched up
like a street of words leading away from her,
  where the Gododdin
marched the Welsh way on the road to oblivion.
So after this emergency there was nothing to be done
but watching her dying, with her vocabulary
leaving her in tides – *nice saucer of tea,*
Nonconformism, hay fever –
and in spite of our efforts, by dawn
her circulation was slow, her lips pale,
the last drops glittering. And that was that.'

Through an extended comparison between the protracted death throes of a language and those of a human body, Gwyneth Lewis is emphasising how intimately integral is a first language to the core being of its speaker. In this poem the incontinent secretions characteristic of dying are not those of bodily fluids but symptoms of verbal dissolution. In one way they are random phrases – their utterance is involuntary and nonsensical. But each phrase is also a significant cultural marker. In the mind of the speaker, language experiences its own kind of dementia, and brings more and more fragments of its vigorous youth back to meaningless life. The result is a kind of inventory of loss. Some phrases are celebrated lines that occur in the heroic poetry of the earliest period of Welsh history; others are rich dialect sayings and pungent proverbs; yet others are garbled memories of a once-powerful religious culture.

And as the quotation marks indicate, there is a witness present at this scene, who is helpless to intervene. Except of course through the act of writing this poem. In it a leading bilingual poet of modern Wales implicitly

acknowledges her responsibility to postpone as far as may be humanly possible the demise of the older of the two languages she speaks – the first-born of the two, in more senses than one. The poem is therefore both a requiem for a language and a pledge to delay its death for as long as may be humanly possible .

When the topic is the death of a language, the translation of the poem into the very language that is responsible for its 'murder' becomes a fraught issue. But then, the Welsh language is as yet very far indeed from being dead – Gwyneth Lewis's poem is the most vivid possible testimony to its contemporary richness and power. And so, the English version may be best thought of as an admirable, and potentially productive, attempt not to consign Welsh to a premature grave but to alert English-speaking readers to its remarkable longevity and resourceful vitality while also carrying the warning that it nevertheless remains a cultural asset that is as rare and precious as it is endangered.

The Final Voyage

There is a long, venerable tradition of poets writing tribute elegies for other poets. One of the most celebrated of those written in the twentieth century was W. H. Auden's 'In Memory of W. B. Yeats'. Particularly moving is its summary of the helpless fate of all dead writers: to be 'scattered among a hundred cities/ And wholly given over to unfamiliar affections'. Yeats died on the very brink of the Second World War. Over half a century later R. S. Thomas died on the very brink of a new century and a new millennium. And in both their cases, it came subsequently to seem as if their deaths had marked a fateful turning point in human affairs.

Rowan Williams is a longstanding admirer of R. S. Thomas. It comes as no surprise, therefore, that he should have wanted to commemorate him in fitting fashion. He duly fashioned the following elegy out of an eclectic mix of spiritual and cultural materials, as if wishing to ensure his poem would acknowledge the decidedly heterodox character of the beliefs of this most turbulent and most restlessly searching of Anglican priests.

ROWAN WILLIAMS (1950–)

Deathship

The last years, words from a window
smoothing the sea, the iron back and forth
to probe the fugitive wrinkles
carving a path down to the lost gate.

What hid in the pale clefts till now
feels for the light, a soft uncertain
fingering as if through
stone, through furrows of flint.

The tides pressed neat as for an evening out:
time to drag down a black boat from the shed,
off through the gate, to balance
on the slow sea at dark ready to sail.

The smoke will rise, the cloudy pillar
wavering across the sky's long page,
At dawn, somewhere westward,
the boat flares in a blaze of crying birds.

The mixing of elements is there in the last two stanzas. In the dragging of the boat out of shed, there is the hint of the launching of a Viking long-boat (Rowan Williams once wryly noted there was something of the fierce axe-wielder about the forbidding, aggressively outspoken character of Thomas); with that there comes a reminder (in the flaring of a boat caught in the rays of a dying sun) of the Viking practice of burying their warrior-leaders in long boats that were then set ablaze; but the black boat is also reminiscent of the frail coracles in which the intrepid Celtic Saints set sail to Christianise Europe; and of course in that mention of smoke and cloud there is an obvious allusion to the wanderings of the Israelites in the wilderness en route to Canaan, guided only by God's pillar of cloud by day and of fire at night. As for the ironing out of the waves, it is reminiscent of Jesus's action in stilling the waters of the Sea of Galilee.

And there is one other possible intriguing allusion, this time to D. H. Lawrence's 'The Ship of Death':

Already the dark and endless ocean of the end
is washing in through the breaches of our wounds,
already the flood is upon us.

Oh build your ship of death, your little ark
and furnish it with food, with little cakes, and wine
for the dark flight down oblivion.

Lawrence's poem views human death as a stage in the natural cycle of decay, death, and rebirth. It ends by imagining the soul's re-emergence into a realm of peace. It, too, is based on the Viking ritual of placing a warrior's body in a long boat, which was set alight and then allowed to drift seawards on the waves. After Thomas's retirement, premature and somewhat embittered, from his last parish at Aberdaron, it was to the natural world around him that he turned for healing and for inspiration.

He had retired to live in a small ancient cottage built of boulders situated on the rocky south coast of the Llŷn Peninsula – that bough of land suspended between sea and air, as he described it. It was there that he wrote some of his most notable spiritual poems, and the most restlessly searching. From the small window of his cottage he looked out over the waters, notoriously treacherous and frequently

stormy, of the bay named Porth Neigwl, known in English as Hell's Mouth – very much to Thomas's amusement. He spent most of his days tramping the surrounding countryside, eyes peeled for birds – he was an avid 'twitcher'. So, by imagining Thomas at the outset smoothing the waves as he probes the sea's 'fugitive wrinkles' and then concluding by imagining his boat disappearing from sight in a 'blaze of crying birds', Rowan Williams is able to take his bearings on Thomas the poet by identifying those features in the physical landscape that represented the two poles of his creative imagination.

In this elegy, Rowan Williams resolutely resists any temptation to write a conventional Christian elegy replete with customary consolations. As he well knew, Thomas did not believe in personal immortality. Indeed, he had refused Christian burial in favour of cremation, and so the reference to the burning ship of a 'pagan' Viking is apposite. The tone that Williams adopts likewise resists any hint of sentimentality. His is instead a touching respect for the flinty resolution with which his fellow-priest had faced up to the difficulties of maintaining any kind of spiritual faith in the modern world. And, by concluding with references to the pillar of smoke by day and fire by

night that guided the ancient Israelites to the Promised Land, Williams implicitly figures Thomas as a kind of Moses of our age, bravely venturing forth to make contact with the infinitely mysterious and remote God of his own distinctive faith. It is a moving tribute to a unique pilgrim soul.

No Sunlight Guest

On 13 June 2005, Joan and Dannie Abse were travelling along the M4, a short distance from their home in Ogmore, when their car was involved in a bad accident, in which Joan was killed. She and her husband had been married for over half a century, and Dannie Abse was left utterly bereft. Herself intellectually gifted, and a fine writer about art, she had also been Dannie's mainstay. He liked to tell the story 'of his young son, David, entering his study with a friend. He pointed out a row of books, all by his father. "Do you see those books over there?" asked David. Abse quickened with pride. "My Mum typed all of them."' After her unexpected, violent passing, Abse likened his condition to that described by the American poet Stanley Moss: 'night is always present, sunlight is the guest.' He just 'limped along.' He wrote the following poem some eighteen months after Joan's death, when he was 81.

DANNIE ABSE (1923–2014)

The Violin Player

Too often now, half somnolent, I would go
like Yeats to a fortunate Lake Isle where
unblemished water-lilies never die
and no solitary swan floats by
from everlasting to everlasting.

And in the tranquil orchard of this Isle
I'd plunder such paradisal apples
that Cézanne could have painted – apples
no bird would have dared to peck at,
fraudulent but beautiful.

Yes, I would go there rapt, recreant,
and stay there because sweet, you're not here
till, self-scolded, I would recollect
my scruffy odorous Uncle Isidore
(surely one of the elect) who played

unsettling, attenuated music
long after a string had snapped,
whose beard bent down to interject,
'Little boy, who needs all the lyric strings?
Is the great world perfect?'

Through recalling Yeats' familiar poem 'The Lake Isle of Innisfree' Abse manages to capture the natural yearning of a mourner to escape to some magical space out of reach of the pain of loss. In that mention of the fruit, perfect as if plucked from one of Cézanne's renowned paintings of still life, there is a poignant covert allusion to Joan, the connoisseur of art, as if she has the power to find him out even in his refuge from grief. Another layer of significance is added in the indirect reference to the famous ancient anecdote about the Greek painter Zeuxis who painted grapes so life-like that the birds descended to peck at them. By contrast, Abse imagines fruit like Cézanne's, that look luscious yet at the same time do not conceal their 'fraudulence'.

That aside about self-scolding, however, anticipates the poem's conclusion. There Abse relates a typically wry Jewish anecdote about his venerable Uncle Isidore by way of a challenge to himself abandon his Innisfree dream, so seductive yet so barren with illusion, and to muster the determination to just keep limping painfully but resolutely along.

Acknowledgements

Excerpt from Dic Jones, 'Galarnad', *Sgubo'r Storws: Pedwaredd Cyfrol o Gerddi* (Llandysul: Gomer, 1986). Reprinted by permission of Y Lolfa.

Excerpt from Elizabeth Bishop, 'One Art', *Poems*, published by Chatto & Windus. Copyright © 2011 by The Alice H. Methfessel Trust. Publisher's Note and compilation copyright © 2011 by Farrar, Straus and Giroux. Reprinted by permission of Farrar, Straus and Giroux, and The Random House Group Limited. All Rights Reserved.

Lewis Glyn Cothi, 'Marwnad Siôn o'r Glyn': Thomas Parry, ed., *The Oxford Book of Welsh Verse* (Oxford: Oxford University Press, reprint, 1998).

Robert Williams (Robert ap Gwilym Ddu), 'Awdl Goffa am ei Ferch': Thomas Parry, ed., *The Oxford Book of Welsh Verse* (Oxford: Oxford University Press, reprint, 1998).

R. Williams Parry, 'Hedd Wyn': Thomas Parry, ed., *The Oxford Book of Welsh Verse* (Oxford: Oxford University Press, reprint, 1998). Reprinted by permission of Y Lolfa.

Alun Lewis, 'Raiders' Dawn': Cary Archard, ed., *Alun Lewis: Collected Poems* (Bridgend: Seren Books, 1994).

Menna Elfyn, 'Angladd' and translation: *Eucalyptus* (Llandysul: Gwasg Gomer, 1999). Reprinted by permission of the author.

Ruth Bidgood, 'All Souls': Ruth Bidgood, *Selected Poems* (Bridgend: Seren, 1992). Reprinted by permission of Ruth Bidgood's estate.

Leslie Norris, 'Elegy for David Beynon'. Copyright © 1969 by Leslie Norris. Appeared in Leslie Norris, *Collected Poems* (Bridgend: Seren, 1996). Reprinted by permission of Brandt & Hochman Literary Agents, Inc. All rights reserved.

Tony Conran, 'Elegy for the dead in the Falkland Islands, 1982': Tony Conran, *The Shape of My Country* (Llanrwst: Gwasg Carreg Gwalch, 2004). Reprinted by permission of Tony Conran's estate.

John Ormond, 'After a death': John Ormond, *Selected Poems* (Bridgend: Seren, 1987). Reprinted by permission of John Ormond's estate.

Gwyneth Lewis, 'Y Munudau Olaf' / 'The Last Minutes': Robert Minhinnick, ed., *The Adulterer's Tongue* (Manchester: Carcanet, 2003). 'Y Munudau Olaf' reprinted by permission of Barddas. 'The Last Minutes' translated by Robert Minhinnick, reprinted by permission of Carcanet.

Rowan Williams, 'Deathship,' *The Poems of Rowan Williams* (Manchester: Carcanet, 2002, 2014 edition). Reprinted by permission of Carcanet.

Dannie Abse, 'The Violin Player', *The Presence* (London: Hutchinson, 2008). Reprinted by permission of Parthian.

Warm thanks to my friend and distinguished novelist Stevie Davies for her invaluable advice during the preparation of this text.